# Deep Learning Explained

## Applications, Challenges, and Opportunities

By Oluchi Ike

# Preface

Deep learning is one of the most transformative technologies of the 21st century, reshaping industries, driving scientific breakthroughs, and redefining how we interact with machines. This book, *Deep Learning Explained: Applications, Challenges, and Opportunities*, is designed for anyone seeking to demystify the concepts of deep learning and explore its real-world applications, as well as its challenges and future potential.

Through detailed explanations, practical examples, and expert insights, this book bridges the gap between complex theories and accessible understanding. Whether you're a student, researcher, industry professional, or an enthusiast of artificial intelligence, this book provides the knowledge you need to navigate the dynamic field of deep learning.

The chapters are organized to build from foundational concepts to advanced applications and challenges. Along the way, you'll discover how deep learning is applied in fields like healthcare, finance, autonomous vehicles, and beyond. You'll also gain an understanding of the ethical, technical, and societal challenges that come with its adoption.

Let's embark on this journey to uncover the incredible world of deep learning and explore its limitless opportunities.

# Table of Contents

## Chapter 1: Introduction to Deep Learning

- 1.1 What is Deep Learning?
- 1.2 Historical Evolution of Neural Networks
- 1.3 Why Deep Learning Matters Today
- 1.4 Key Components of a Deep Learning System

## Chapter 2: Neural Network Basics

- 2.1 The Anatomy of Neural Networks
- 2.2 Activation Functions Explained
- 2.3 Types of Neural Networks
- 2.4 Training Neural Networks

## Chapter 3: Deep Learning Frameworks and Tools

- 3.1 Overview of Popular Frameworks (TensorFlow, PyTorch, etc.)
- 3.2 Data Preprocessing for Deep Learning
- 3.3 Model Deployment and Optimization
- 3.4 Open Source Resources and Libraries

## Chapter 4: Applications in Computer Vision

- 4.1 Image Classification
- 4.2 Object Detection and Segmentation

- 4.3 Generative Adversarial Networks (GANs) in Vision
- 4.4 Challenges in Computer Vision

**Chapter 5: Applications in Natural Language Processing**

- 5.1 Sentiment Analysis and Text Classification
- 5.2 Machine Translation
- 5.3 Text Summarization
- 5.4 Chatbots and Conversational AI

**Chapter 6: Applications in Healthcare**

- 6.1 Medical Image Analysis
- 6.2 Drug Discovery
- 6.3 Personalized Medicine
- 6.4 Ethical Concerns in AI-Powered Healthcare

**Chapter 7: Applications in Finance and Business**

- 7.1 Fraud Detection
- 7.2 Algorithmic Trading
- 7.3 Customer Insights with Deep Learning
- 7.4 Risk Management

**Chapter 8: Reinforcement Learning and Robotics**

- 8.1 Basics of Reinforcement Learning
- 8.2 Deep Reinforcement Learning Applications

- 8.3 Robotics and Automation
- 8.4 Challenges in Reinforcement Learning

**Chapter 9: Challenges in Deep Learning**

- 9.1 The Need for Large Datasets
- 9.2 Computational Power and Costs
- 9.3 Interpretability of Deep Learning Models
- 9.4 Addressing Bias in Deep Learning

**Chapter 10: Opportunities and Future Directions**

- 10.1 Emerging Trends in Deep Learning
- 10.2 AI for Social Good
- 10.3 Industry Innovations and Case Studies
- 10.4 Bridging Research and Practical Applications

**Chapter 11: Ethical and Societal Implications**

- 11.1 Privacy and Security Concerns
- 11.2 Bias and Fairness in AI Systems
- 11.3 Regulations and Policy Development
- 11.4 Building Trustworthy AI Systems

**Chapter 12: Theoretical Foundations**

- 12.1 Gradient Descent and Backpropagation
- 12.2 Optimization Techniques

- 12.3 Regularization and Generalization
- 12.4 Understanding Overfitting

## Chapter 13: Case Studies in Deep Learning

- 13.1 Autonomous Vehicles
- 13.2 Smart Assistants
- 13.3 AI in Agriculture
- 13.4 The Role of Deep Learning in Smart Cities

## Chapter 14: Learning Deep Learning

- **14.1 Resources for Beginners**
- **14.2 Intermediate and Advanced Learning Paths**
- **14.3 Building Your First Deep Learning Model**
- **14.4 Final Thoughts and Next Steps**

# Chapter 1: Introduction to Deep Learning

## 1.1 What is Deep Learning?

Deep learning is a subset of artificial intelligence (AI) and machine learning (ML) that focuses on training artificial neural networks to recognize patterns and solve complex problems. At its core, deep learning mimics the way the human brain processes information by creating interconnected layers of nodes (neurons) that work together to analyze data. Unlike traditional machine learning algorithms, which often require manual feature engineering, deep learning models can automatically extract relevant features from raw data. This ability to learn representations from unstructured data such as images, text, and audio has made deep learning a transformative technology across numerous industries.

The "deep" in deep learning refers to the depth of the neural networks, which consist of multiple layers. Each layer processes the input data to extract increasingly abstract features. For example, in an image recognition task, the initial layers might identify edges and colors, while deeper layers recognize shapes and objects. This hierarchical learning process allows deep learning models to achieve remarkable accuracy in tasks like image classification, speech recognition, and natural language processing (NLP).

## 1.2 Historical Evolution of Neural Networks

The journey of neural networks and deep learning began decades ago, long before the term "deep learning" became mainstream. In the 1940s, Warren McCulloch and Walter Pitts proposed the first computational model of a neuron, laying the groundwork for artificial neural networks. Their model demonstrated that a simple network of neurons could compute logical functions, sparking interest in mimicking biological intelligence.

In the 1950s and 1960s, Frank Rosenblatt developed the perceptron, a simple neural network capable of binary classification. Although promising, the perceptron was limited to solving linearly separable problems, as highlighted in Marvin Minsky and Seymour Papert's 1969 book *Perceptrons*. This limitation led to a period of stagnation known as the "AI Winter."

The revival of neural networks began in the 1980s with the introduction of backpropagation, a method for efficiently training multi-layer networks. Researchers like Geoffrey Hinton, David Rumelhart, and Ronald Williams demonstrated that backpropagation could enable neural networks to learn from data, reigniting interest in the field. However, progress was still hindered by limited computational power and small datasets.

In the 2000s, deep learning entered a new era with breakthroughs in computational capabilities, the availability of large datasets, and algorithmic advancements. Key milestones included the development of convolutional neural networks (CNNs) for image recognition and recurrent neural networks (RNNs) for sequence data. In 2012, Alex Krizhevsky's AlexNet achieved unprecedented accuracy in the ImageNet competition, marking the beginning of deep learning's dominance in AI research. Today, deep learning is a cornerstone of AI, with applications ranging from self-driving cars to healthcare diagnostics.

**1.3 Why Deep Learning Matters Today**

Deep learning has become a game-changer in AI, enabling machines to perform tasks once thought impossible. Its significance lies in its ability to process and learn from vast amounts of data, uncovering patterns and insights that would be challenging for humans to discern.

One of the most compelling reasons deep learning matters today is its versatility. Unlike traditional algorithms tailored for specific tasks, deep learning models can be adapted to a wide range of applications. For instance, the same underlying principles used in speech recognition systems can be applied to medical imaging, fraud detection, or even video game development.

Deep learning's capacity for automation is another critical factor. By automating feature extraction and decision-making processes, deep learning reduces the need for manual intervention, accelerating innovation in industries like finance, retail, and logistics. In healthcare, for example, deep learning algorithms assist in diagnosing diseases, predicting patient outcomes, and personalizing treatments, all with remarkable precision.

Moreover, deep learning's ability to handle unstructured data makes it invaluable in an era dominated by social media, IoT devices, and big data. Unstructured data, which includes images, text, and audio, constitutes the majority of information generated today. Deep learning excels at processing such data, enabling breakthroughs in areas like sentiment analysis, natural language understanding, and real-time translation.

As AI becomes increasingly embedded in our daily lives, deep learning drives progress in fields like autonomous vehicles, smart assistants, and virtual reality. Its transformative potential extends to addressing global challenges, such as climate change, education, and public health, making it a cornerstone of technological advancement.

## 1.4 Key Components of a Deep Learning System

A deep learning system comprises several interconnected components, each playing a crucial role in the model's success. Understanding these components is essential for building, training, and deploying deep learning models.

1. **Data**: Data is the foundation of any deep learning system. High-quality, diverse, and adequately labeled datasets are necessary to train models

effectively. For instance, image recognition tasks require annotated images, while NLP applications rely on large text corpora. Data preprocessing, such as normalization, augmentation, and tokenization, ensures the input data is suitable for model training.

2. **Neural Networks**: At the heart of deep learning systems are neural networks, consisting of layers of interconnected nodes. Each layer performs a specific transformation on the input data, extracting features and passing them to subsequent layers. Neural networks can be customized for different tasks, such as CNNs for visual data and RNNs for sequential data.

3. **Training Process**: Training involves optimizing the neural network's parameters using algorithms like gradient descent and backpropagation. The model learns to minimize a loss function, which measures the difference between its predictions and the actual labels. Hyperparameter tuning, such as selecting the learning rate and batch size, ensures efficient and effective training.

4. **Hardware and Software**: Deep learning's computational demands necessitate specialized hardware like GPUs and TPUs, which accelerate matrix operations and parallel computations. Software frameworks such as TensorFlow, PyTorch, and Keras provide tools for building and deploying models, offering user-friendly interfaces and robust libraries.

5. **Evaluation and Deployment**: After training, the model's performance is evaluated using metrics like accuracy, precision, and recall. Deployment involves integrating the trained model into real-world applications, ensuring it operates efficiently and reliably. Continuous monitoring and updates are necessary to maintain performance and adapt to changing conditions.

By understanding the fundamentals of deep learning, its historical evolution, and its key components, readers can appreciate the transformative power of this technology and its potential to shape the future. The next chapter will delve deeper into the structure and mechanics of neural networks, the building blocks of deep learning systems.

## Chapter 2: Neural Network Basics

### 2.1 The Anatomy of Neural Networks

A neural network is a computational system inspired by the structure and functionality of the human brain. At its core, a neural network consists of interconnected layers of nodes or neurons, where each node performs a mathematical operation. These networks process input data through successive layers, extracting meaningful patterns or features that help achieve a specific task, such as classifying images or predicting numerical values.

The three main components of a neural network are:

1. **Input Layer**: The input layer serves as the network's entry point, receiving raw data that the model will analyze. Each node in this layer corresponds to one feature or variable in the dataset. For example, in an image recognition task, the input layer might represent the pixel values of an image.

2. **Hidden Layers**: Hidden layers sit between the input and output layers, forming the network's processing core. Each layer transforms its input data through weighted connections and activation functions. The number of hidden layers and nodes depends on the complexity of the task. In deep learning, networks with multiple hidden layers are referred to as "deep" networks, enabling the model to capture more intricate patterns.

3. **Output Layer**: The output layer generates the network's predictions or classifications. For example, in a binary classification problem, the output layer might contain a single neuron that outputs a value between 0 and 1, representing the probability of belonging to a specific class.

In addition to these layers, neural networks rely on **weights** and **biases**, which adjust the strength of connections between neurons, and **activation functions**, which introduce non-linearity into the model. Together, these components enable neural networks to model complex relationships in data.

## 2.2 Activation Functions Explained

Activation functions are critical to the functionality of neural networks, introducing non-linear transformations that allow the network to learn and model complex data relationships. Without activation functions, a neural network would behave like a simple linear model, severely limiting its capacity to solve real-world problems.

Here are some commonly used activation functions:

1. **Sigmoid Function**: The sigmoid function maps inputs to a range between 0 and 1, making it ideal for binary classification problems. Its formula is:

$$\text{Sigmoid}(x) = \frac{1}{1 + e^{-x}}$$

While useful, the sigmoid function suffers from the vanishing gradient problem, which can hinder the training of deep networks.

2. **ReLU (Rectified Linear Unit)**: ReLU is the most widely used activation function in deep learning due to its simplicity and efficiency. It outputs the input directly if positive and zero otherwise:

$$\text{ReLU}(x) = \max(0, x)$$

ReLU addresses the vanishing gradient problem, but it can suffer from "dead neurons," where certain nodes become inactive during training.

3. **Tanh (Hyperbolic Tangent)**: The tanh function maps inputs to a range between -1 and 1, making it a centered activation function. Its formula is:

$$\text{Tanh}(x) = \frac{e^x - e^{-x}}{e^x + e^{-x}}$$

Tanh is often preferred over sigmoid because its outputs are zero-centered, but it still encounters vanishing gradient issues in deep networks.

4. **Softmax**: The softmax function is commonly used in the output layer of classification networks. It converts logits (raw predictions) into probabilities that sum to 1, allowing the network to assign confidence scores to each class.

Activation functions are essential for enabling neural networks to model non-linear relationships and make accurate predictions in complex tasks.

## 2.3 Types of Neural Networks

Neural networks come in various architectures, each designed for specific tasks. Understanding these types helps in selecting the appropriate model for a given problem.

1. **Feedforward Neural Networks (FNNs)**: These are the simplest type of neural network, where data flows in one direction—from the input layer to the output layer—without any cycles or feedback loops. FNNs are ideal for tasks like regression and basic classification.

2. **Convolutional Neural Networks (CNNs)**: CNNs are specialized for image and spatial data processing. They use convolutional layers to extract features like edges, textures, and shapes from images. CNNs are widely used in image recognition, object detection, and video analysis.

3. **Recurrent Neural Networks (RNNs)**: RNNs are designed for sequential data, where the current output depends on previous inputs. They include feedback loops that allow information to persist, making them suitable for tasks like time series analysis and natural language processing.

4. **Generative Adversarial Networks (GANs)**: GANs consist of two networks—a generator and a discriminator—that compete with each other. The generator creates fake data, while the discriminator tries to distinguish between real and fake data. GANs are used in image generation, style transfer, and synthetic data creation.

5. **Transformer Networks**: Transformers have revolutionized natural language processing by using self-attention mechanisms to handle long-range dependencies in data. They are the backbone of models like BERT and GPT, which excel in text understanding and generation.

## 2.4 Training Neural Networks

Training a neural network involves teaching it to map input data to desired outputs by optimizing its weights and biases. The training process can be broken into several key steps:

1. **Forward Propagation**: During this step, input data is passed through the network, and predictions are generated. The output is compared to the actual labels to calculate the loss, which measures the model's performance.

2. **Loss Function**: The loss function quantifies the difference between predicted and actual values. Common loss functions include mean squared error (MSE) for regression and cross-entropy loss for classification.

3. **Backpropagation**: Backpropagation adjusts the network's weights and biases by calculating gradients of the loss function with respect to each parameter. This process uses the chain rule of calculus to propagate errors backward through the network.

4. **Optimization**: Optimization algorithms, like stochastic gradient descent (SGD) or Adam, use the gradients to update the weights and biases. These updates aim to minimize the loss function and improve model accuracy.

5. **Validation and Tuning**: A portion of the data, called the validation set, is used to evaluate the model's performance during training. Hyperparameters, such as the learning rate and batch size, are fine-tuned to optimize results.

Training neural networks requires balancing computational resources, data quality, and model complexity to achieve high performance and generalization.

---

With a solid understanding of neural network anatomy, activation functions, types, and training processes, readers are prepared to explore the advanced techniques and applications that define deep learning's versatility and power. The next chapter will delve into the critical role of data preparation and preprocessing in ensuring the success of deep learning models.

# Chapter 3: Deep Learning Frameworks and Tools

## 3.1 Overview of Popular Frameworks

Deep learning frameworks provide developers with the tools and infrastructure to build, train, and deploy models efficiently. They abstract the complexities of matrix operations, gradient calculations, and hardware optimizations, allowing researchers and practitioners to focus on model design and experimentation. Two of the most popular frameworks are **TensorFlow** and **PyTorch**, though several other frameworks cater to various needs.

1. **TensorFlow**: Developed by Google, TensorFlow is a versatile and widely adopted deep learning framework. Known for its scalability, it can be used for both research and production-level deployment. TensorFlow's key features include:

    - **Keras API**: A high-level interface for building and training models.
    - **TensorBoard**: A visualization tool for tracking model performance and debugging.
    - **TF Lite**: Optimized for deploying models on mobile and edge devices. TensorFlow supports a variety of languages, including Python, C++, and JavaScript, making it suitable for diverse applications.

2. **PyTorch**: PyTorch, developed by Facebook, is favored for its flexibility and dynamic computational graph. It allows developers to adjust models on the fly, making it particularly appealing to researchers. PyTorch features:

    - **TorchScript**: Enables transitioning between research and production.

- **ONNX (Open Neural Network Exchange)**: Allows interoperability between frameworks.
- **Ease of Debugging**: Its Pythonic nature and straightforward syntax make it beginner-friendly.

3. **Other Frameworks**:
    - **Keras**: Originally a standalone library, Keras is now integrated with TensorFlow. It is popular for its user-friendly interface and rapid prototyping capabilities.
    - **MXNet**: Backed by Apache, MXNet is known for its efficiency and support for multiple programming languages.
    - **Caffe**: Designed for speed, Caffe is ideal for image processing tasks and applications requiring low-latency predictions.
    - **JAX**: Developed by Google, JAX is gaining traction for its performance in numerical computing and deep learning tasks, leveraging automatic differentiation.

Each framework has strengths tailored to specific use cases, whether you're conducting exploratory research or deploying models at scale.

## 3.2 Data Preprocessing for Deep Learning

Data preprocessing is a critical step in the deep learning pipeline. Poor data quality can compromise the performance of even the most sophisticated models. The goal of preprocessing is to clean, transform, and structure data so that it can be fed into a neural network effectively.

1. **Data Cleaning**:

- **Handling Missing Values**: Replace missing entries with appropriate values (mean, median, or mode) or remove affected data points.
- **Outlier Detection**: Identify and handle outliers that could distort the model's understanding. Techniques like Z-score or IQR (Interquartile Range) are often used.

2. **Normalization and Standardization**:
   - **Normalization**: Rescales data to a specific range, such as [0, 1], ensuring that features contribute equally during training.
   - **Standardization**: Centers data around the mean with a standard deviation of one, making it suitable for algorithms sensitive to scale.

3. **Data Augmentation**:
   - Data augmentation artificially expands the dataset by applying transformations such as rotation, scaling, flipping, or cropping to images or sequences. This technique enhances the model's ability to generalize.

4. **Encoding Categorical Data**:
   - **One-Hot Encoding**: Converts categorical variables into binary arrays.
   - **Label Encoding**: Assigns a unique integer to each category.

5. **Splitting Data**:
   Divide data into training, validation, and test sets to evaluate and prevent overfitting. A common split is 70% training, 15% validation, and 15% testing.

Data preprocessing ensures that input data is structured and relevant, paving the way for effective model training.

## 3.3 Model Deployment and Optimization

Once a deep learning model is trained, the next step is deployment—making the model available for real-world use. Deployment involves converting the model into an operational format and optimizing it for efficiency.

1. **Model Conversion**:

    Convert trained models into formats compatible with deployment environments. Examples include TensorFlow SavedModel, ONNX, or CoreML.

2. **Inference Optimization**:

    - **Quantization**: Reduces model size by using lower-precision data types (e.g., converting 32-bit floating-point to 8-bit integers).

    - **Pruning**: Eliminates redundant parameters without significantly affecting accuracy.

    - **Model Compression**: Compresses the model to fit within hardware constraints, such as on mobile or edge devices.

3. **Deployment Platforms**:

    - **Cloud Services**: Platforms like AWS, Google Cloud AI, and Microsoft Azure provide scalable environments for model hosting.

    - **Edge Devices**: Deploy models on devices like smartphones, IoT sensors, or autonomous vehicles using frameworks like TensorFlow Lite or PyTorch Mobile.

    - **Web Applications**: Use JavaScript-based frameworks like TensorFlow.js for browser-based deployment.

4. **Monitoring and Maintenance**:

    Continuous monitoring ensures the model remains accurate and reliable. If the model's performance deteriorates, retraining with updated data may be necessary.

Model deployment transforms a static experiment into a dynamic application, making deep learning accessible to end-users.

## 3.4 Open Source Resources and Libraries

The deep learning community thrives on open-source contributions. These resources accelerate development by providing pre-built tools, datasets, and codebases.

1. **Libraries for Preprocessing and Analysis**:
    - **NumPy**: Fundamental for numerical computing.
    - **Pandas**: Provides powerful tools for data manipulation.
    - **Matplotlib and Seaborn**: Visualization libraries to analyze and interpret data.

2. **Model Implementation Libraries**:
    - **Hugging Face Transformers**: Offers pre-trained models for natural language processing tasks.
    - **OpenCV**: Specialized in image and video processing.
    - **scikit-learn**: Contains machine learning algorithms for tasks like clustering and classification.

3. **Open Datasets**:
    - **ImageNet**: A large-scale dataset for image classification.
    - **COCO (Common Objects in Context)**: Focuses on object detection and segmentation.

- **Kaggle**: Hosts a variety of datasets across domains.

4. **Community Resources**:
    - **GitHub**: A hub for open-source projects and repositories.
    - **Papers with Code**: Combines academic research with open-source implementations.

These resources and tools empower practitioners to innovate and implement deep learning solutions efficiently.

---

With an understanding of the frameworks, preprocessing techniques, deployment strategies, and open-source resources, practitioners are well-equipped to build and deploy robust deep learning systems. The next chapter will explore the importance of data in more detail, covering strategies for collection, augmentation, and efficient storage.

# Chapter 4: Applications in Computer Vision

Computer vision, a key domain of deep learning, focuses on enabling machines to interpret and understand visual information from the world. From identifying objects in an image to generating entirely new visuals, the applications of deep learning in computer vision are vast and transformative. This chapter delves into some of the most impactful applications and highlights the challenges faced in this domain.

## 4.1 Image Classification

Image classification is one of the foundational tasks in computer vision. It involves assigning a label to an image from a predefined set of categories. For instance, given an image of a dog, the model classifies it under the "dog" category.

Deep learning revolutionized image classification with the advent of **convolutional neural networks (CNNs)**. CNNs excel at automatically extracting hierarchical features from images, significantly outperforming traditional hand-crafted feature methods.

**Key Applications**:

- **Medical Imaging**: Classifying X-rays, MRIs, or CT scans to identify conditions like pneumonia, cancer, or fractures.
- **Facial Recognition**: Identifying individuals for security and authentication purposes.
- **Autonomous Vehicles**: Detecting road signs or hazards for navigation.

Popular architectures like AlexNet, VGGNet, ResNet, and EfficientNet have pushed the boundaries of accuracy and efficiency in image classification. However, challenges like class imbalance, data augmentation, and explainability remain areas of active research.

## 4.2 Object Detection and Segmentation

While image classification determines what an image contains, **object detection** and **segmentation** go further by identifying and localizing multiple objects in an image.

1. **Object Detection**:
   Object detection algorithms predict bounding boxes around detected objects and label them. Frameworks like YOLO (You Only Look Once), SSD (Single Shot MultiBox Detector), and Faster R-CNN have become standard tools for real-time and high-accuracy detection.

   **Applications**:
   - **Surveillance**: Detecting suspicious activity or intrusions.
   - **Retail**: Tracking inventory and monitoring customer behavior in stores.
   - **Agriculture**: Identifying pests or assessing crop health through drone imagery.

2. **Image Segmentation**:
   Segmentation is categorized into two types:
   - **Semantic Segmentation**: Assigns a label to each pixel in an image, grouping regions into categories (e.g., sky, trees, road).
   - **Instance Segmentation**: Differentiates between individual instances of the same object category (e.g., distinguishing between two dogs in the same image).

   **Applications**:
   - **Healthcare**: Segmenting tumors in medical scans.

- **Autonomous Driving**: Understanding road layouts and obstacles.
- **AR/VR**: Enhancing experiences by segmenting and overlaying virtual objects on real-world environments.

The success of detection and segmentation tasks hinges on robust algorithms, large labeled datasets (e.g., COCO, Pascal VOC), and effective data augmentation to improve model generalization.

### 4.3 Generative Adversarial Networks (GANs) in Vision

Generative Adversarial Networks (GANs) represent a paradigm shift in computer vision by enabling machines to generate realistic images. GANs consist of two neural networks:

- **Generator**: Creates synthetic data resembling real data.
- **Discriminator**: Distinguishes between real and generated data. Through adversarial training, both networks improve iteratively, producing high-quality outputs.

**Applications of GANs in Vision:**

1. **Image Synthesis**: GANs can create photorealistic images from scratch, such as generating human faces that don't exist in reality.
2. **Image-to-Image Translation**: Tasks like converting sketches into realistic images, turning black-and-white photos into color, or transforming day scenes into night scenes.
    - Example: **Pix2Pix** and **CycleGAN** frameworks.
3. **Super-Resolution**: Enhancing the resolution of low-quality images for applications like satellite imagery and medical scans.

- Example: GAN-based models like **SRGAN**.

4. **Style Transfer**: Combining artistic styles with photographs, such as applying the style of Van Gogh to a modern cityscape.

5. **Data Augmentation**: Generating diverse samples to augment datasets for training more robust models.

Despite their versatility, GANs are challenging to train due to issues like mode collapse (when the generator produces limited diversity) and instability during training.

## 4.4 Challenges in Computer Vision

The remarkable achievements in computer vision come with their share of challenges. Understanding and addressing these hurdles is essential to pushing the boundaries of what is possible.

1. **Data Quality and Quantity**:
    - Deep learning models require vast amounts of labeled data. Obtaining high-quality annotations can be time-consuming and expensive.
    - Datasets often suffer from biases, leading to models that perform poorly on underrepresented categories or groups.

2. **Generalization**:
    - Models trained on specific datasets may struggle when applied to different environments. For instance, a pedestrian detection model trained on urban streets may fail in rural areas.
    - Domain adaptation techniques and transfer learning aim to mitigate this issue but are not foolproof.

3. **Computational Demands**:

- Training state-of-the-art models requires significant computational resources, such as GPUs and TPUs, which may not be accessible to everyone.
- Deployment on edge devices like smartphones or IoT sensors demands efficient, lightweight models.

4. **Ethical Concerns**:
   - **Privacy**: Applications like surveillance and facial recognition raise questions about data privacy and misuse.
   - **Bias**: Models can inherit biases present in training data, leading to unfair or discriminatory outcomes.

5. **Real-Time Processing**:
   - Applications like autonomous vehicles and real-time surveillance demand low-latency predictions, which are challenging to achieve without sacrificing accuracy.

6. **Interpretability**:
   - Deep learning models are often described as "black boxes." Understanding why a model makes a specific decision is crucial, especially in sensitive applications like healthcare or criminal justice.

Despite these challenges, advancements in techniques like unsupervised learning, federated learning, and explainable AI are paving the way for more robust, ethical, and scalable computer vision systems.

---

Computer vision's integration into diverse industries underscores its transformative potential. From recognizing objects and generating images to addressing complex real-world challenges, deep learning continues to drive innovation. The next chapter will explore applications in natural language processing, another pivotal domain reshaped by deep learning technologies.

## Chapter 5: Applications in Natural Language Processing

Natural Language Processing (NLP) is a subfield of artificial intelligence (AI) focused on the interaction between computers and human language. It enables machines to understand, interpret, and generate human language in a way that is both meaningful and useful. With the rapid advancements in deep learning, NLP has become a cornerstone of modern AI applications. This chapter explores some of the key applications of deep learning in NLP, including sentiment analysis, machine translation, text summarization, and chatbots/conversational AI.

### 5.1 Sentiment Analysis and Text Classification

Sentiment analysis is one of the most widely used applications of NLP, where the goal is to determine the sentiment expressed in a piece of text—whether it is positive, negative, or neutral. This technique is especially useful for businesses to gauge customer opinions from reviews, social media posts, and other textual content.

#### Deep Learning in Sentiment Analysis

Traditional sentiment analysis methods relied on rule-based systems or machine learning models like Naive Bayes and Support Vector Machines (SVM). However, deep learning models, especially recurrent neural networks (RNNs) and transformers, have taken sentiment analysis to new levels of accuracy by capturing complex contextual relationships in text.

- **Recurrent Neural Networks (RNNs)**, particularly long short-term memory (LSTM) networks, are effective in processing sequential data, like sentences, where the meaning depends on the sequence of words.
- **Transformers**, such as BERT (Bidirectional Encoder Representations from Transformers) and GPT (Generative Pretrained Transformer), have

revolutionized sentiment analysis by enabling bidirectional understanding of text, allowing models to capture context from both sides of a word in a sentence.

**Applications of Sentiment Analysis:**

- **Customer Feedback**: Companies can analyze product reviews, customer surveys, and social media comments to understand consumer sentiment and improve their offerings.

- **Market Research**: Analysts use sentiment analysis to gauge public opinion on market trends, political events, or brand perception.

- **Social Media Monitoring**: Sentiment analysis is also used to track public sentiment on topics like political campaigns or social issues.

Text classification, on the other hand, involves categorizing text into predefined labels. It is widely used in email filtering, spam detection, and topic modeling. Both tasks leverage similar deep learning models for high accuracy, often utilizing techniques such as CNNs and transformers to classify text effectively.

## 5.2 Machine Translation

Machine translation (MT) is the process of automatically translating text or speech from one language to another. Traditional rule-based and statistical translation systems often struggled to capture the nuances and complexity of human languages. Deep learning, particularly neural machine translation (NMT), has significantly improved the quality and fluency of translations.

**Neural Machine Translation (NMT)**

NMT systems use deep learning models, primarily sequence-to-sequence (seq2seq) architectures, which consist of an encoder-decoder structure. The **encoder** reads the source language text and converts it into a fixed-length vector, and the **decoder** generates the translation in the target language. Transformers have further enhanced NMT by allowing models to consider all words in a sentence simultaneously, rather than sequentially, which improves translation accuracy.

- **Attention Mechanism**: Introduced in transformer models like BERT and GPT, attention mechanisms allow the model to focus on specific words in a sentence, improving translation quality by maintaining context, even in long sentences.

- **Pretrained Models**: Models like Google's **BERT**, Facebook's **M2M-100**, and OpenAI's **GPT-3** have revolutionized MT by enabling multilingual translation without relying on direct parallel training for every language pair.

**Applications of Machine Translation:**

- **Cross-Language Communication**: NMT allows for real-time communication between speakers of different languages, which is essential for businesses expanding into global markets.

- **Content Localization**: Websites, applications, and multimedia content are translated to local languages, allowing companies to reach international audiences effectively.

- **Multilingual Support**: Translation systems help provide multilingual customer support, helping businesses offer assistance across different regions.

While NMT has made great strides, challenges remain, particularly with low-resource languages where training data is scarce. Additionally, cultural nuances, idioms, and context-specific expressions can sometimes lead to inaccurate translations.

**5.3 Text Summarization**

Text summarization involves condensing long documents or articles into shorter, more digestible versions, retaining the most important information. It is a valuable tool for information retrieval, content curation, and knowledge management. Text summarization is typically divided into two types: extractive and abstractive summarization.

1. **Extractive Summarization**:

    Extractive summarization selects key phrases, sentences, or paragraphs directly from the source text. While it's relatively easy to implement, it sometimes results in summaries that are disjointed or lack coherence.

2. **Abstractive Summarization**:

    Abstractive summarization generates entirely new sentences that convey the most important information, much like how a human would summarize a text. Deep learning models such as transformers (e.g., GPT, BERT) have improved abstractive summarization by learning to paraphrase content while maintaining its meaning.

**Deep Learning for Summarization**

Deep learning models like **BART** (Bidirectional and Auto-Regressive Transformers) and **T5** (Text-to-Text Transfer Transformer) have demonstrated state-of-the-art performance in abstractive summarization tasks. These models can handle large and complex text sources, generating concise and coherent summaries. The encoder-decoder architecture of these models allows them to understand the content and generate accurate summaries, improving readability and retaining critical details.

**Applications of Text Summarization**:

- **News Aggregation**: Summarizing news articles and reports, enabling readers to quickly grasp key points.

- **Legal and Medical Documents**: Summarizing lengthy contracts, reports, or research papers to assist professionals in understanding essential information.

- **Content Discovery**: Providing quick summaries for large-scale data repositories, such as academic papers, business documents, and books.

While text summarization has advanced significantly, ensuring accuracy, coherence, and readability remains a challenge, particularly in abstractive methods.

## 5.4 Chatbots and Conversational AI

Chatbots and conversational AI systems have become ubiquitous in customer service, healthcare, education, and other sectors. These systems are designed to simulate human conversation and provide automated assistance to users. Deep learning has played a pivotal role in advancing the capabilities of chatbots, making them more natural, responsive, and context-aware.

### Deep Learning in Chatbots

Earlier chatbots were based on rule-based systems, which responded to specific inputs with pre-programmed answers. However, deep learning, particularly with models like **transformers** and **seq2seq** networks, has enabled more sophisticated conversational agents. These models learn from vast amounts of conversational data to generate contextually relevant responses.

- **Context Awareness**: Deep learning models can track context and manage multi-turn conversations, enabling more coherent interactions over extended dialogues.

- **Intent Recognition**: Models can understand user intentions beyond surface-level keywords and provide more accurate responses.

- **Personalization**: With continuous learning, conversational agents can tailor responses based on user preferences and previous interactions.

**Applications of Conversational AI:**

- **Customer Support**: Chatbots handle inquiries, troubleshoot issues, and provide recommendations 24/7.

- **Healthcare**: Virtual assistants offer medical information, schedule appointments, and assist with basic diagnoses.

- **E-commerce**: Chatbots guide users through the shopping experience, providing product recommendations and assisting with checkouts.

- **Education**: AI-powered tutors assist students with learning, answer questions, and offer personalized feedback.

Despite their success, challenges like handling ambiguous queries, ensuring ethical interactions, and maintaining privacy remain significant considerations in the development of conversational AI systems.

---

The application of deep learning in NLP has transformed how machines interact with human language, opening up new possibilities for communication, information processing, and automation. The future of NLP holds exciting potential as researchers continue to push the boundaries of what is possible with language models. The next chapter will explore the applications of deep learning in speech recognition, another vital aspect of human-computer interaction.

## Chapter 6: Applications in Healthcare

Healthcare is one of the most promising fields for the application of deep learning. With its ability to analyze large datasets, identify patterns, and make predictions, deep learning has revolutionized various aspects of medicine, from diagnostics to treatment planning. This chapter delves into the transformative applications of deep learning in healthcare, including medical image analysis, drug discovery, personalized medicine, and the ethical challenges posed by AI in the medical field.

---

### 6.1 Medical Image Analysis

Medical imaging is an essential diagnostic tool, providing critical insights into patient health through modalities such as X-rays, CT scans, MRIs, and ultrasounds. Deep learning has significantly enhanced the analysis of medical images, offering improved accuracy and efficiency in detecting abnormalities and diseases.

**Automated Diagnosis and Detection**

Deep learning models, particularly convolutional neural networks (CNNs), are highly effective in processing and analyzing medical images. These models can detect diseases like cancer, neurological disorders, and cardiovascular conditions with remarkable precision.

- **Cancer Detection**: CNNs are widely used for identifying tumors in mammograms, lung CT scans, and skin lesion images. Models trained on large datasets can identify malignancies at an early stage, often outperforming human radiologists in accuracy.
- **Neurological Disorders**: Deep learning aids in diagnosing conditions such as Alzheimer's and Parkinson's disease by analyzing brain scans.

- **Cardiology**: Algorithms can interpret echocardiograms and detect heart abnormalities, aiding cardiologists in making accurate diagnoses.

**Segmentation and Localization**

Deep learning also enables precise segmentation and localization of anatomical structures. For instance, models can delineate the boundaries of tumors, organs, and other features, facilitating targeted treatments like radiotherapy.

**Challenges in Medical Image Analysis:**

While the results are promising, challenges persist, including data privacy concerns, the need for high-quality annotated datasets, and the generalizability of models across diverse patient populations.

---

## 6.2 Drug Discovery

Drug discovery is a resource-intensive process that traditionally takes years of research and billions of dollars. Deep learning has emerged as a game-changing tool, accelerating drug development by identifying potential candidates, optimizing chemical structures, and predicting drug-target interactions.

**Molecule Generation and Optimization**

Deep generative models, such as variational autoencoders (VAEs) and generative adversarial networks (GANs), are used to design novel molecules with specific properties. These models can generate thousands of molecular structures, significantly speeding up the initial stages of drug discovery.

**Target Identification and Validation**

Deep learning models help identify potential biological targets for new drugs by analyzing genomic and proteomic data. Models can predict how a drug will interact with a target, helping researchers prioritize compounds for further testing.

### Clinical Trial Optimization

Deep learning is also transforming clinical trials by analyzing patient data to identify suitable candidates, predict outcomes, and optimize trial design. This reduces costs and increases the likelihood of success.

### Challenges in Drug Discovery:

Despite its promise, the application of deep learning in drug discovery faces hurdles such as limited access to high-quality data, the complexity of biological systems, and regulatory requirements for drug approval.

## 6.3 Personalized Medicine

Personalized medicine aims to tailor medical treatments to the individual characteristics of each patient, such as genetic makeup, lifestyle, and environment. Deep learning has become a cornerstone of personalized medicine by enabling precise predictions and recommendations based on patient-specific data.

### Genomic Analysis

Deep learning models analyze genomic data to identify genetic variants associated with diseases. This allows for early diagnosis and personalized treatment plans, particularly in oncology, where treatments like immunotherapy are tailored to the genetic profile of the patient's tumor.

### Predictive Analytics

By analyzing electronic health records (EHRs), wearable device data, and other sources, deep learning can predict patient outcomes, such as the likelihood of developing a chronic condition. These predictions enable proactive interventions and better health management.

### Optimizing Treatment Plans

Deep learning assists in optimizing treatment plans by simulating how patients might respond to various therapies. For example, models can predict the effectiveness of different drug combinations for individual patients, reducing trial-and-error approaches in treatment.

### Challenges in Personalized Medicine:

The adoption of deep learning in personalized medicine is constrained by data privacy issues, the need for interoperable healthcare systems, and the ethical considerations of using AI to make life-altering decisions.

---

## 6.4 Ethical Concerns in AI-Powered Healthcare

While the applications of deep learning in healthcare hold immense promise, they also raise significant ethical challenges. As AI-powered systems become integral to medical practice, addressing these concerns is critical to ensuring equitable and safe healthcare delivery.

### Bias in Algorithms

Deep learning models can inherit biases present in training data, leading to disparities in care. For example, a model trained on data from predominantly one demographic may not perform well for others, potentially exacerbating healthcare inequities.

### Transparency and Explainability

Deep learning models often operate as "black boxes," making it difficult for healthcare professionals to understand the reasoning behind their predictions. This lack of transparency can hinder trust and acceptance among clinicians and patients.

### Data Privacy and Security

Healthcare data is highly sensitive, and the use of deep learning raises concerns about data privacy and security. Ensuring compliance with regulations like HIPAA (Health Insurance Portability and Accountability Act) and implementing robust encryption protocols are essential for protecting patient information.

**Accountability and Liability**

When AI systems make errors, determining accountability becomes complex. Questions arise about who is responsible—the developers, the healthcare providers, or the system itself. Establishing clear guidelines for liability is critical to addressing these issues.

**Ethical Use of AI**

The use of AI in areas like genetic analysis and predictive analytics raises ethical questions about consent, the potential misuse of data, and the societal implications of AI-driven healthcare decisions. For example, predicting the likelihood of developing a disease could lead to discrimination in insurance or employment.

---

Deep learning has the potential to revolutionize healthcare, offering unprecedented opportunities for improving diagnosis, treatment, and patient outcomes. However, its successful integration into medical practice requires addressing technical, regulatory, and ethical challenges. As we move forward, collaboration between technologists, healthcare professionals, policymakers, and ethicists will be crucial in harnessing the full potential of deep learning while safeguarding human well-being.

The next chapter will explore how deep learning is transforming the field of autonomous systems, particularly in robotics and self-driving vehicles.

**Chapter 7: Applications in Finance and Business**

Deep learning has become a cornerstone in modern finance and business, providing sophisticated tools for data analysis, decision-making, and risk assessment. By leveraging its ability to process complex datasets, identify patterns, and make accurate predictions, deep learning is reshaping how businesses operate and manage financial systems. In this chapter, we explore the transformative applications of deep learning in fraud detection, algorithmic trading, customer insights, and risk management.

## 7.1 Fraud Detection

Fraud is a persistent challenge in the finance industry, costing billions of dollars annually. Traditional rule-based systems for detecting fraudulent activities often fall short due to their inability to adapt to evolving threats. Deep learning, with its advanced pattern-recognition capabilities, offers a dynamic solution to combating fraud.

**Anomaly Detection**

Deep learning models, such as autoencoders and recurrent neural networks (RNNs), are adept at identifying unusual patterns in transactional data. By analyzing massive datasets in real-time, these models can flag suspicious activities like unauthorized credit card transactions or unusual login behaviors.

- **Credit Card Fraud**: Deep learning systems can analyze transaction histories, geolocation, and purchasing patterns to detect anomalies that may indicate fraud.

- **Insurance Fraud**: In the insurance sector, deep learning algorithms analyze claim data and detect patterns indicative of fraudulent activities, such as exaggerated claims or repeated incidents.

**Adaptive Learning**

Unlike traditional systems that require manual updates to rules and thresholds, deep learning models continuously learn and adapt to new types of fraud. This makes them particularly effective in dealing with sophisticated cyber threats like phishing and social engineering attacks.

**Challenges in Fraud Detection:**

While deep learning enhances fraud detection, it also faces challenges, including the need for high-quality labeled data, the risk of false positives, and the complexity of interpreting model predictions for regulatory compliance.

---

## 7.2 Algorithmic Trading

Algorithmic trading, also known as quantitative or algo trading, relies heavily on data-driven models to make split-second decisions in financial markets. Deep learning has significantly improved the accuracy and efficiency of trading algorithms, enabling them to process vast amounts of data and identify profitable opportunities.

**Market Prediction**

Deep learning models like long short-term memory (LSTM) networks and attention mechanisms are used to predict market trends by analyzing historical price data, news sentiment, and macroeconomic indicators. These models excel in capturing temporal dependencies, making them ideal for time-series forecasting.

**Portfolio Optimization**

Deep reinforcement learning is increasingly being used for portfolio optimization.

These models simulate various market scenarios and learn strategies to maximize returns while minimizing risks.

**High-Frequency Trading**

Deep learning also powers high-frequency trading (HFT) systems that execute trades in milliseconds. By analyzing real-time market data, these systems can identify arbitrage opportunities and execute trades faster than human traders.

**Challenges in Algorithmic Trading**:

The use of deep learning in trading comes with challenges, including the need for low-latency infrastructure, the risk of overfitting to historical data, and regulatory scrutiny over algorithmic practices.

---

## 7.3 Customer Insights with Deep Learning

Understanding customer behavior is crucial for businesses to deliver personalized experiences and drive growth. Deep learning enables organizations to analyze customer data at scale, providing actionable insights that can enhance engagement and loyalty.

**Sentiment Analysis**

Deep learning models analyze customer reviews, social media posts, and survey responses to gauge sentiment. For instance, natural language processing (NLP) models can identify whether customers are satisfied, dissatisfied, or neutral about a product or service.

**Personalization**

Deep learning drives personalized recommendations by analyzing customer preferences and behaviors. Retailers like Amazon and streaming platforms like Netflix use recommendation systems powered by deep learning to suggest products or content tailored to individual users.

- **E-Commerce**: By analyzing clickstream data, deep learning models can predict what a customer is likely to purchase next, enabling targeted marketing campaigns.
- **Banking**: In finance, deep learning helps segment customers based on their spending habits, enabling banks to offer personalized financial products.

**Churn Prediction**

Deep learning models can predict customer churn by identifying patterns that indicate dissatisfaction or disengagement. Businesses can then take proactive measures, such as offering discounts or improving services, to retain at-risk customers.

**Challenges in Customer Insights:**

While deep learning enhances customer insights, challenges include ensuring data privacy, avoiding algorithmic bias, and maintaining transparency in decision-making processes.

## 7.4 Risk Management

Risk management is a critical function in finance and business, involving the identification, assessment, and mitigation of potential risks. Deep learning provides advanced tools for risk analysis, helping organizations make informed decisions and safeguard their assets.

**Credit Risk Assessment**

Deep learning models analyze vast amounts of customer data, including credit history, income levels, and spending habits, to assess creditworthiness. This enables financial institutions to make more accurate lending decisions and reduce default rates.

**Market Risk Analysis**

Deep learning is used to model and predict market risks by analyzing factors like volatility, interest rates, and geopolitical events. These models provide early warnings of potential downturns, enabling organizations to take preemptive actions.

**Operational Risk Management**

Operational risks, such as system failures or cyberattacks, are increasingly being managed using deep learning. Models can predict system vulnerabilities and recommend measures to strengthen security protocols.

**Stress Testing and Scenario Analysis**

Deep learning enhances stress testing by simulating various economic scenarios and evaluating their impact on an organization's financial health. This helps businesses prepare for adverse events and ensure compliance with regulatory requirements.

**Challenges in Risk Management:**

Implementing deep learning in risk management involves challenges such as ensuring model interpretability, dealing with incomplete or biased data, and integrating AI-driven insights with traditional risk management frameworks.

---

Deep learning has become a vital tool for addressing complex challenges in finance and business. From fraud detection to risk management, its applications offer unparalleled accuracy and efficiency, enabling organizations to stay competitive in an increasingly data-driven world. However, as with any technology, its successful implementation requires addressing ethical, regulatory, and technical challenges.

The next chapter will explore how deep learning is driving innovation in autonomous systems, including robotics and self-driving vehicles.

## Chapter 8: Reinforcement Learning and Robotics

Reinforcement learning (RL) is a dynamic and rapidly evolving field of artificial intelligence that focuses on training agents to make decisions by interacting with their environment. Combined with deep learning, RL has unlocked significant advancements in robotics and automation, enabling machines to perform complex tasks and adapt to real-world challenges. In this chapter, we delve into the basics of reinforcement learning, its applications in various domains, the role it plays in robotics and automation, and the challenges it faces.

---

### 8.1 Basics of Reinforcement Learning

Reinforcement learning is a machine learning paradigm where an agent learns to perform actions in an environment to maximize cumulative rewards. Unlike supervised learning, which relies on labeled data, RL uses a trial-and-error approach to discover optimal strategies.

### Core Concepts of RL

1. **Agent**: The decision-maker in the system (e.g., a robot, algorithm).
2. **Environment**: The world in which the agent operates.
3. **State (S)**: The current situation of the environment.
4. **Action (A)**: Choices available to the agent in a given state.
5. **Reward (R)**: Feedback received after performing an action.

### Markov Decision Process (MDP)

Reinforcement learning is often modeled as an MDP, characterized by:

- **States**: Representing the environment at a specific point.
- **Actions**: The set of choices available to the agent.
- **Transition Probabilities**: The likelihood of moving from one state to another after taking an action.
- **Rewards**: Numerical feedback for actions performed in the environment.

### Exploration vs. Exploitation

A fundamental challenge in RL is balancing exploration (trying new actions to discover better rewards) with exploitation (leveraging known actions to maximize rewards). Algorithms like epsilon-greedy address this trade-off by introducing randomness to the agent's decision-making process.

---

### 8.2 Deep Reinforcement Learning Applications

Deep reinforcement learning (DRL) enhances RL by integrating deep neural networks, enabling agents to handle high-dimensional environments and complex tasks. DRL has applications across various industries:

### Game Playing

DRL has gained widespread attention through its success in mastering games like chess, Go, and video games. Algorithms like AlphaGo and AlphaZero use DRL to achieve superhuman performance by learning strategies from scratch.

### Autonomous Vehicles

In self-driving cars, DRL helps in decision-making processes like lane changes, obstacle avoidance, and navigation. By simulating real-world scenarios, agents learn to handle dynamic traffic environments effectively.

### Healthcare

DRL is being used to optimize treatment strategies, personalize drug dosages, and manage complex diseases like cancer. Agents can simulate patient responses and recommend optimal treatment paths.

### Energy Management

Smart grids utilize DRL to optimize energy distribution, reduce costs, and balance demand and supply. RL algorithms ensure efficient use of renewable energy resources like solar and wind.

---

## 8.3 Robotics and Automation

Reinforcement learning has revolutionized robotics by enabling machines to learn from interactions and adapt to uncertain environments.

### Skill Acquisition

RL allows robots to acquire new skills through practice and feedback. For instance, a robot arm can learn to grasp objects by experimenting with different angles and grip forces.

### Path Planning and Navigation

Mobile robots use RL to navigate complex terrains, avoiding obstacles and finding optimal paths. Applications range from warehouse automation to planetary exploration.

### Human-Robot Collaboration

In industrial settings, RL-powered robots collaborate with humans to perform tasks like assembly, welding, and quality inspection. These robots learn to adjust their behavior based on human feedback.

### Sim-to-Real Transfer

Robots are often trained in simulated environments before being deployed in the real world. RL algorithms facilitate this "sim-to-real" transfer by enabling robots to generalize learned behaviors to new contexts.

### Automation in Manufacturing

RL enhances automation in manufacturing by optimizing processes such as predictive maintenance, supply chain management, and production scheduling. This reduces downtime and increases efficiency.

---

## 8.4 Challenges in Reinforcement Learning

Despite its successes, reinforcement learning faces several challenges that limit its widespread adoption.

### Sample Efficiency

RL algorithms often require millions of interactions with the environment to converge to an optimal policy. This is particularly challenging for real-world applications where data collection is expensive or time-consuming.

### Reward Engineering

Designing a reward function that accurately reflects the desired outcome is critical. Poorly designed reward functions can lead to unintended behaviors, such as an agent exploiting loopholes in the system.

### Exploration in Complex Environments

Exploring high-dimensional or sparse environments can be daunting for RL agents. Techniques like curiosity-driven learning and intrinsic motivation are being developed to address this issue.

**Computational Requirements**

Training RL models is computationally intensive, often requiring specialized hardware like GPUs or TPUs. This poses a barrier for small-scale organizations or individuals with limited resources.

**Safety and Robustness**

In safety-critical applications like healthcare and autonomous vehicles, ensuring that RL agents perform reliably under varying conditions is paramount. Adversarial attacks and unexpected inputs can compromise system performance.

**Ethical Considerations**

The deployment of RL systems in areas like surveillance, autonomous weapons, and social interactions raises ethical questions about accountability, bias, and the potential misuse of technology.

---

Reinforcement learning has opened new frontiers in artificial intelligence, driving innovations in robotics, automation, and beyond. By enabling machines to learn from their environment and adapt to challenges, RL offers immense potential to transform industries. However, addressing its limitations is essential to unlocking its full capabilities and ensuring responsible deployment.

The next chapter will focus on how deep learning is advancing the field of autonomous systems, exploring its applications in self-driving vehicles, drones, and intelligent robotics.

# Chapter 9: Challenges in Deep Learning

While deep learning has transformed industries and opened new frontiers in artificial intelligence, it is not without its challenges. From the need for large datasets to the lack of interpretability in models, these obstacles must be addressed for deep learning to reach its full potential. This chapter explores the critical challenges in deep learning, focusing on data requirements, computational costs, interpretability, and bias.

---

## 9.1 The Need for Large Datasets

Deep learning models excel in tasks such as image recognition, natural language processing, and predictive analytics due to their ability to learn complex patterns. However, these capabilities come at the cost of requiring massive datasets.

**Why Large Datasets Are Essential**

Deep neural networks consist of millions, sometimes billions, of parameters. To train these parameters effectively and avoid overfitting, models require diverse and comprehensive datasets. For instance, an image recognition model needs thousands of labeled images for each category to generalize well.

**Challenges in Data Collection**

1. **Availability**: In many domains, especially healthcare and finance, obtaining large datasets is difficult due to privacy concerns and proprietary restrictions.

2. **Annotation**: Data labeling is labor-intensive and costly. Crowdsourcing platforms like Amazon Mechanical Turk provide solutions, but the quality of annotations can vary.

3. **Data Imbalance**: In many datasets, certain classes are underrepresented, leading to biased models. Techniques like data augmentation and synthetic data generation help but are not foolproof.

**Potential Solutions**

1. **Transfer Learning**: Pre-trained models on large datasets can be fine-tuned for specific tasks, reducing the need for extensive data.

2. **Unsupervised and Semi-Supervised Learning**: Techniques that leverage unlabeled data are becoming increasingly popular.

3. **Synthetic Data**: Simulated data, such as GAN-generated images, can supplement real-world datasets.

---

## 9.2 Computational Power and Costs

Training deep learning models is computationally intensive, often requiring specialized hardware and significant financial resources.

**Hardware Requirements**

1. **GPUs and TPUs**: Graphics Processing Units (GPUs) and Tensor Processing Units (TPUs) are the backbone of deep learning. However, they are expensive, with high-end GPUs costing thousands of dollars.

2. **Memory and Storage**: Large datasets and models require substantial memory and storage, further increasing infrastructure costs.

**Energy Consumption**

Training deep models consumes enormous amounts of energy, raising concerns about the environmental impact. For example, training a single deep learning model can emit as much carbon dioxide as five cars over their lifetimes.

**Potential Solutions**

1. **Model Compression**: Techniques like pruning, quantization, and knowledge distillation reduce the size of models without sacrificing performance.

2. **Cloud Computing**: Platforms like AWS, Google Cloud, and Microsoft Azure offer scalable computing resources, making deep learning more accessible.

3. **Green AI**: Efforts to design energy-efficient algorithms and hardware are gaining momentum, emphasizing sustainability in AI research.

---

## 9.3 Interpretability of Deep Learning Models

Deep learning models are often criticized as "black boxes" due to their lack of transparency. Understanding how models arrive at their predictions is crucial, especially in high-stakes domains like healthcare, finance, and autonomous vehicles.

**Why Interpretability Matters**

1. **Trust**: Users and stakeholders need to trust model decisions, particularly when lives or finances are at risk.

2. **Debugging**: Identifying and correcting errors in models is challenging without interpretability.

3. **Regulation**: Legal frameworks, such as the EU's GDPR, require explainable AI systems.

**Challenges in Interpretability**

1. **Complex Architectures**: The layered and non-linear nature of deep networks makes them inherently opaque.

2. **Trade-Offs**: Improving interpretability often comes at the expense of model performance.

**Techniques for Interpretability**

1. **Feature Importance**: Methods like SHAP (SHapley Additive exPlanations) and LIME (Local Interpretable Model-agnostic Explanations) help identify which features contribute most to predictions.

2. **Visualization**: Tools like activation maps and saliency plots provide visual insights into model behavior.

3. **Simplified Models**: Surrogate models approximate complex models to explain their decisions in simpler terms.

---

## 9.4 Addressing Bias in Deep Learning

Bias in deep learning models is a critical issue that can perpetuate or even amplify societal inequalities. From facial recognition systems that perform poorly on certain demographics to biased hiring algorithms, the implications are profound.

**Sources of Bias**

1. **Data Bias**: If the training data reflects societal biases, the model will learn and propagate those biases. For instance, a hiring algorithm trained on data from a predominantly male workforce may favor male candidates.

2. **Algorithmic Bias**: Even unbiased data can lead to biased outcomes due to the design of the model or optimization process.

3. **Human Bias**: Bias can be introduced during data collection, annotation, or model evaluation.

**Consequences of Bias**

1. **Fairness**: Biased models can lead to unfair treatment, particularly for marginalized groups.

2. **Reputation**: Organizations deploying biased AI systems face public backlash and loss of trust.

3. **Legal and Ethical Risks**: Non-compliance with anti-discrimination laws and ethical standards can result in legal repercussions.

**Strategies to Mitigate Bias**

1. **Diverse Datasets**: Ensuring diversity in training data minimizes the risk of bias.

2. **Fairness Metrics**: Tools like IBM's AI Fairness 360 assess and mitigate bias in models.

3. **Human Oversight**: Involving diverse teams in data preparation and model evaluation helps identify potential biases.

4. **Bias Correction Algorithms**: Techniques like re-weighting, re-sampling, and adversarial debiasing aim to reduce model bias.

---

**Conclusion**

Addressing the challenges in deep learning is critical for its continued growth and adoption. While the need for large datasets, computational power, interpretability, and bias mitigation present significant hurdles, researchers and practitioners are actively developing innovative solutions. By overcoming these challenges, deep learning can continue to revolutionize industries and unlock new possibilities in artificial intelligence.

The next chapter will explore how scalability and distributed systems enable the training and deployment of large-scale deep learning models, highlighting the tools and techniques driving this progress.

## Chapter 10: Opportunities and Future Directions

As deep learning continues to evolve, its potential for transformative impact grows exponentially. This chapter explores the emerging trends, societal benefits, industry innovations, and efforts to bridge the gap between research and practical applications in deep learning. These opportunities and future directions provide a roadmap for leveraging the technology to solve complex problems and unlock new possibilities.

### 10.1 Emerging Trends in Deep Learning

The field of deep learning is constantly advancing, with new trends and methodologies reshaping its landscape.

**Self-Supervised Learning**
Self-supervised learning has gained traction as a way to train models on unlabeled data, significantly reducing the dependence on costly and time-consuming data labeling. This approach allows models to learn useful representations by predicting parts of the data from other parts, making it especially valuable in domains with limited labeled datasets, such as healthcare and scientific research.

**Transformers Beyond NLP**
Initially designed for natural language processing (NLP), transformer architectures are now being applied in diverse fields like computer vision (Vision Transformers) and protein structure prediction. Their ability to model long-range dependencies and process sequential data has opened new avenues for innovation.

**Federated Learning**
Privacy concerns are a significant barrier to AI adoption in industries like healthcare and finance. Federated learning addresses this by enabling models to be trained on

decentralized data across multiple devices or locations without sharing sensitive information.

**Quantum Machine Learning**

As quantum computing matures, its integration with deep learning offers the promise of solving problems that are currently computationally intractable. Although still in its infancy, quantum machine learning could revolutionize fields such as cryptography, optimization, and drug discovery.

**Sustainability in AI**

Efforts to make deep learning more energy-efficient are gaining momentum. Techniques like low-rank approximation, model pruning, and energy-efficient hardware design are becoming critical for reducing the environmental impact of AI systems.

---

**10.2 AI for Social Good**

Deep learning has immense potential to address societal challenges and improve the quality of life.

**Healthcare Accessibility**

AI-powered diagnostic tools are being deployed in remote and underserved areas to provide healthcare access to populations that lack traditional medical infrastructure. For example, deep learning models can analyze X-rays or detect diseases from smartphone images, enabling early diagnosis and intervention.

**Disaster Management**

Deep learning is being used to predict natural disasters, such as floods and earthquakes, and to optimize emergency response strategies. Satellite imagery analysis helps identify disaster-prone areas and assess the impact of events in real-time.

### Education and Literacy

AI-driven tools are improving education by personalizing learning experiences, providing real-time feedback, and making educational content accessible in multiple languages. For instance, language translation tools powered by deep learning are breaking down barriers for students in non-native language settings.

### Environmental Conservation

Deep learning is aiding wildlife conservation efforts by analyzing images from camera traps, detecting illegal fishing activities, and optimizing renewable energy resources. Climate models enhanced by AI are improving the accuracy of weather predictions and tracking environmental changes.

---

## 10.3 Industry Innovations and Case Studies

The adoption of deep learning across industries is driving remarkable innovations and success stories.

### Autonomous Vehicles

Deep learning is the cornerstone of self-driving car technologies. Companies like Tesla and Waymo use convolutional neural networks (CNNs) for object detection, semantic segmentation, and trajectory prediction, enabling vehicles to navigate complex environments safely.

### Retail and E-commerce

Retailers leverage deep learning for customer personalization, dynamic pricing, and inventory management. Recommendation systems powered by deep neural networks have become a key driver of sales in e-commerce platforms like Amazon and Netflix.

### Agriculture

Precision agriculture is benefiting from deep learning applications that analyze drone imagery to monitor crop health, detect pests, and optimize irrigation systems. These advancements help farmers increase yields while minimizing environmental impact.

**Manufacturing**

In manufacturing, deep learning improves quality control through automated defect detection and predictive maintenance, reducing downtime and costs. Robots equipped with deep learning algorithms are revolutionizing assembly lines by adapting to new tasks autonomously.

## 10.4 Bridging Research and Practical Applications

Despite the advancements in deep learning research, the gap between theoretical innovation and real-world implementation remains a challenge. Bridging this divide is essential for maximizing the benefits of deep learning.

**Collaboration Between Academia and Industry**

Fostering partnerships between academic researchers and industry practitioners accelerates the translation of cutting-edge research into practical applications. Joint initiatives, conferences, and open innovation platforms facilitate knowledge sharing and collaborative problem-solving.

**Standardization and Benchmarking**

Standardizing datasets, evaluation metrics, and deployment protocols ensures consistency and reproducibility in deep learning applications. Benchmarking tools like ImageNet and GLUE provide common ground for researchers and developers to assess progress.

**Scalable Deployment Strategies**

For deep learning to be widely adopted, models need to be scalable and accessible.

Cloud-based platforms, edge computing, and containerization technologies like Docker and Kubernetes make it easier to deploy AI solutions at scale.

**Ethical Frameworks**

As deep learning systems become more pervasive, ethical considerations must guide their development and deployment. Establishing clear guidelines for privacy, bias mitigation, and accountability ensures that AI systems serve the broader interests of society.

---

**Conclusion**

The opportunities in deep learning are as vast as its challenges are complex. Emerging trends like self-supervised learning, transformers, and federated learning promise to reshape industries, while applications in healthcare, education, and environmental conservation demonstrate the technology's potential for social good.

The future of deep learning lies in fostering collaboration, standardization, and ethical practices. By bridging the gap between research and practical applications, deep learning can continue to drive innovation, address global challenges, and unlock unprecedented opportunities across all sectors of society.

In the next chapter, we will explore scalability and distributed systems in deep learning, focusing on how to train and deploy models efficiently in large-scale environments.

**Chapter 11: Ethical and Societal Implications**

Deep learning technologies have become pervasive in modern society, shaping industries and influencing daily life. However, with great power comes significant responsibility. This chapter delves into the ethical and societal implications of deep learning, focusing on key areas like privacy, bias, regulatory frameworks, and building trustworthy AI systems. These considerations are vital to ensuring that the benefits of deep learning are realized without compromising fundamental human rights and values.

## 11.1 Privacy and Security Concerns

One of the most pressing issues in deep learning is the protection of privacy and security in data-intensive environments.

### Data Privacy Challenges

Deep learning models often rely on vast amounts of data to function effectively. However, this reliance raises concerns about the privacy of individuals whose data is collected, stored, and processed. For instance, facial recognition systems and personalized recommendation engines may inadvertently collect sensitive information, exposing users to privacy violations.

### Security Vulnerabilities

Deep learning models are not immune to cyberattacks. Adversarial attacks, where malicious actors subtly alter input data to mislead models, pose significant risks. For example, a slight modification to an image could trick a facial recognition system into misidentifying an individual. Additionally, data breaches involving sensitive datasets used in training can have far-reaching consequences, including identity theft and financial fraud.

### Solutions and Mitigations

To address these concerns, organizations must adopt robust data protection strategies. Techniques such as differential privacy, federated learning, and data encryption can safeguard user information while maintaining model performance. Transparency in data collection and usage policies is equally crucial for gaining user trust.

## 11.2 Bias and Fairness in AI Systems

Deep learning models are only as unbiased as the data they are trained on, making fairness a critical issue in AI development.

### Sources of Bias

Bias in AI systems often stems from skewed or incomplete training data. For example, a hiring algorithm trained on historical data may inadvertently perpetuate gender or racial biases if those biases were present in the original dataset. Similarly, language models can reflect societal stereotypes embedded in the text corpora used for training.

### Consequences of Bias

Biased AI systems can have serious repercussions, from reinforcing discrimination to eroding public trust. In criminal justice, for instance, biased algorithms could result in unfair sentencing recommendations. In healthcare, inequitable AI tools might overlook or misdiagnose conditions in underrepresented populations.

### Promoting Fairness

Addressing bias requires proactive measures, including diverse and representative datasets, algorithmic audits, and fairness-aware machine learning techniques. Incorporating ethical principles into the development process and involving multidisciplinary teams can further ensure that AI systems uphold fairness and equity.

## 11.3 Regulations and Policy Development

As deep learning becomes more integrated into society, regulatory frameworks are essential to balance innovation with ethical accountability.

**Current Regulatory Landscape**

While some countries have implemented AI-specific regulations, such as the European Union's General Data Protection Regulation (GDPR) and the proposed AI Act, others lag behind. These regulations address issues like data privacy, algorithmic transparency, and accountability, laying the groundwork for ethical AI governance.

**Challenges in Policy Development**

Creating effective regulations for deep learning is complex due to the technology's rapid evolution and cross-border implications. Policymakers must strike a delicate balance between fostering innovation and mitigating risks. Overregulation could stifle progress, while lax policies may lead to unchecked misuse.

**Global Cooperation**

Given the global nature of AI, international cooperation is vital. Organizations like the United Nations and the Organisation for Economic Co-operation and Development (OECD) are working to establish common principles for AI ethics and governance. Collaborative efforts between governments, academia, and industry can help create cohesive and effective regulatory frameworks.

---

## 11.4 Building Trustworthy AI Systems

Trust is the cornerstone of ethical AI adoption, and building trustworthy systems requires a multifaceted approach.

**Transparency and Explainability**

Deep learning models, often criticized as "black boxes," must become more interpretable to gain user trust. Techniques like attention mechanisms, model visualization, and interpretable AI frameworks allow stakeholders to understand how decisions are made, increasing confidence in the technology.

**Robustness and Reliability**

Trustworthy AI systems must be robust and reliable, performing consistently under diverse conditions. Rigorous testing, validation, and monitoring are essential to identify and address potential weaknesses. For instance, stress-testing models with adversarial examples can help developers mitigate vulnerabilities.

**Ethical Design Principles**

Embedding ethical principles into AI design ensures that systems align with societal values. This includes prioritizing user privacy, minimizing harm, and promoting inclusivity. Frameworks like "Ethics by Design" encourage developers to consider ethical implications throughout the AI lifecycle.

**Public Engagement and Education**

Engaging the public in discussions about deep learning's societal impact fosters trust and informed decision-making. Educational initiatives can demystify AI technologies, empowering individuals to understand and evaluate their benefits and risks.

---

## Conclusion

The ethical and societal implications of deep learning are as profound as its technological potential. Privacy and security concerns, biases in AI systems, and the lack of comprehensive regulations pose significant challenges that demand immediate attention. However, these challenges also present opportunities to shape deep learning into a force for good.

By addressing bias, safeguarding privacy, and building trustworthy systems, stakeholders can ensure that deep learning aligns with human values and societal needs. As policymakers, developers, and researchers collaborate on ethical frameworks and governance, the future of deep learning can be both innovative and responsible.

In the next chapter, we will explore scalability and distributed systems in deep learning, focusing on how these technologies can support the growing demands of modern AI applications.

**Chapter 12: Theoretical Foundations**

Understanding the theoretical underpinnings of deep learning is essential for designing, training, and optimizing models effectively. This chapter delves into foundational concepts such as gradient descent, backpropagation, optimization techniques, regularization, generalization, and the challenge of overfitting. These principles form the backbone of modern deep learning methodologies, bridging theory and practical implementation.

---

**12.1 Gradient Descent and Backpropagation**

At the heart of deep learning lies the ability of neural networks to learn from data, a process driven by gradient descent and backpropagation.

**Gradient Descent**

Gradient descent is an optimization algorithm used to minimize the loss function, which measures the difference between predicted and actual outcomes. The algorithm works iteratively, adjusting the model's parameters to reduce errors.

The process involves computing the gradient (partial derivative) of the loss function with respect to each parameter and updating the parameters in the direction opposite to the gradient. The step size for these updates, known as the learning rate, determines how quickly the model converges to a minimum.

Variants of gradient descent include:

- **Batch Gradient Descent**: Processes the entire dataset at once, leading to stable updates but requiring significant computational resources.

- **Stochastic Gradient Descent (SGD)**: Updates parameters for each data point, enabling faster iterations but introducing variability.
- **Mini-Batch Gradient Descent**: Combines the advantages of both, processing small batches of data for more efficient and stable updates.

## Backpropagation

Backpropagation, short for "backward propagation of errors," is the algorithm that computes gradients in neural networks. It involves two steps:

1. **Forward Pass**: The input propagates through the network to compute predictions.
2. **Backward Pass**: The error propagates backward, calculating gradients for each weight and bias.

Backpropagation ensures efficient computation of gradients, enabling deep networks to learn even with millions of parameters.

---

## 12.2 Optimization Techniques

While gradient descent is a cornerstone of training, advanced optimization techniques improve efficiency and convergence.

### Momentum

Momentum accelerates gradient descent by incorporating the past gradients' direction into updates, helping navigate flat or oscillating regions of the loss landscape.

### Adaptive Methods

- **Adagrad**: Adapts the learning rate for each parameter based on the historical gradient, making larger updates for infrequently occurring features.

- **RMSprop**: Addresses Adagrad's diminishing learning rate by introducing an exponentially decaying average of past gradients.

- **Adam (Adaptive Moment Estimation)**: Combines the strengths of momentum and RMSprop, providing adaptive learning rates for faster convergence.

**Learning Rate Scheduling**

Dynamic adjustment of the learning rate during training improves performance. Techniques include step decay, exponential decay, and cyclical learning rates, each tailored to specific training dynamics.

These optimization strategies are critical for training deep networks effectively, reducing computational costs and improving model accuracy.

---

## 12.3 Regularization and Generalization

In deep learning, the goal is not only to fit the training data but also to generalize well to unseen data. Regularization techniques help achieve this balance.

**Regularization Techniques**

1. **L1 and L2 Regularization**

    - **L1 Regularization**: Adds the absolute values of weights to the loss function, encouraging sparsity in the model (many weights become zero).

    - **L2 Regularization**: Adds the squared values of weights, discouraging large weight values and improving stability.

2. **Dropout**

   Dropout randomly deactivates neurons during training, forcing the network to learn redundant representations and reducing overfitting.

3. **Early Stopping**

   Monitoring validation loss during training allows for stopping once performance starts degrading, preventing overfitting.

4. **Data Augmentation**

   Enhancing the training dataset with transformations (e.g., rotations, cropping, flipping) improves the network's robustness and ability to generalize.

## Generalization in Deep Learning

Generalization refers to a model's ability to perform well on unseen data. Factors influencing generalization include model complexity, training data quality, and the effectiveness of regularization techniques.

---

## 12.4 Understanding Overfitting

Overfitting occurs when a model learns the training data too well, capturing noise and irrelevant patterns instead of generalizable features.

### Causes of Overfitting

- **Insufficient Training Data**: Small datasets lead to over-reliance on specific examples.

- **Excessive Model Complexity**: Deep networks with too many parameters can memorize training data.

- **Poor Data Quality**: Noisy or biased datasets exacerbate overfitting.

## Symptoms of Overfitting

A clear indicator of overfitting is a significant gap between training and validation performance. While training loss decreases, validation loss stagnates or worsens.

## Mitigating Overfitting

1. **Regularization Techniques**: Applying L1, L2 regularization, or dropout reduces overfitting risks.

2. **Simplifying Models**: Reducing the number of layers or neurons decreases complexity.

3. **Expanding Datasets**: Acquiring more data or using augmentation enhances generalization.

4. **Cross-Validation**: Splitting data into multiple training-validation subsets ensures robust evaluation and tuning.

## Bias-Variance Tradeoff

Understanding overfitting requires balancing bias (error due to underfitting) and variance (error due to overfitting). Optimal models achieve a harmonious tradeoff, minimizing both.

---

## Conclusion

The theoretical foundations of deep learning—gradient descent, backpropagation, optimization techniques, regularization, and understanding overfitting—are critical for effective model development. Mastery of these principles enables practitioners to train robust, efficient, and generalizable neural networks.

The next chapter will explore scalability and distributed systems, delving into how large-scale systems and parallel computing power modern deep learning frameworks and applications.

## Chapter 13: Case Studies in Deep Learning

Deep learning has evolved from a niche research domain to a transformative technology impacting diverse industries. This chapter presents real-world case studies, showcasing its applications in autonomous vehicles, smart assistants, agriculture, and smart cities. These examples illustrate the tangible impact of deep learning, highlighting its ability to revolutionize systems, improve efficiency, and address critical challenges.

---

### 13.1 Autonomous Vehicles

Autonomous vehicles (AVs), or self-driving cars, represent one of the most ambitious applications of deep learning. The ability to navigate complex environments safely and efficiently relies heavily on the integration of advanced neural networks.

**How Deep Learning Powers Autonomous Vehicles**

1. **Perception**: Deep learning enables vehicles to interpret sensory data, such as images from cameras, LiDAR, and radar. Convolutional Neural Networks (CNNs) identify objects like pedestrians, vehicles, and traffic signs.

2. **Decision-Making**: Reinforcement learning models optimize driving decisions, from lane-keeping to speed adjustment.

3. **Localization and Mapping**: Recurrent Neural Networks (RNNs) and advanced algorithms analyze GPS data and environmental maps for accurate positioning.

**Case in Point: Tesla**

Tesla's Autopilot system employs a vision-based approach, leveraging CNNs trained on millions of miles of driving data. The system enables features like adaptive cruise control, automatic lane changes, and parking assistance.

**Challenges and Future Directions**

- Addressing safety concerns in dynamic environments.
- Enhancing generalization across diverse weather and traffic conditions.
- Overcoming ethical dilemmas in decision-making (e.g., collision scenarios).

## 13.2 Smart Assistants

Smart assistants like Alexa, Siri, and Google Assistant exemplify how deep learning is redefining human-computer interaction. These systems rely on Natural Language Processing (NLP) and speech recognition to deliver seamless conversational experiences.

**Key Technologies Behind Smart Assistants**

1. **Speech Recognition**: Deep learning models convert spoken language into text with high accuracy, utilizing Recurrent Neural Networks (RNNs) and Transformers.

2. **Natural Language Understanding (NLU)**: NLP models extract intent and context from user queries, enabling meaningful responses.

3. **Dialogue Management**: Reinforcement learning optimizes multi-turn conversations by adapting responses based on user feedback.

4. **Personalization**: Recommendation systems powered by deep learning enhance user experiences by tailoring content and suggestions.

**Case in Point: Google Assistant**

Google Assistant uses Transformer-based models like BERT to achieve contextual understanding and natural dialogue. The system integrates seamlessly across devices, offering voice commands for smart home controls, reminders, and more.

**Challenges**

- Improving multi-lingual support and understanding of regional accents.
- Addressing privacy concerns with voice data storage and usage.
- Reducing latency for real-time responses.

## 13.3 AI in Agriculture

Agriculture, a sector crucial to global sustenance, has seen transformative advancements through deep learning. From precision farming to disease detection, neural networks enable smarter, more sustainable agricultural practices.

**Applications of Deep Learning in Agriculture**

1. **Crop Monitoring**: CNNs analyze aerial imagery to assess crop health, identify nutrient deficiencies, and predict yields.

2. **Pest and Disease Detection**: Image classification models identify signs of pest infestations and plant diseases, enabling timely intervention.

3. **Automated Machinery**: Robotics powered by deep reinforcement learning optimize harvesting, planting, and irrigation processes.

4. **Weather Prediction**: Deep learning models analyze meteorological data to provide accurate forecasts, helping farmers make informed decisions.

**Case in Point: Blue River Technology**

Blue River Technology, a subsidiary of John Deere, developed a "See & Spray" system that uses CNNs to identify and target weeds precisely, reducing herbicide use and promoting sustainable farming.

**Challenges and Opportunities**

- Making technology accessible to small-scale farmers.
- Improving the robustness of models for diverse agricultural environments.
- Scaling up data collection for underrepresented regions.

---

## 13.4 The Role of Deep Learning in Smart Cities

As urbanization accelerates, smart cities are leveraging deep learning to enhance livability, sustainability, and efficiency. These systems integrate IoT (Internet of Things) devices with AI to address urban challenges.

**Applications of Deep Learning in Smart Cities**

1. **Traffic Management**: CNNs and RNNs analyze real-time traffic data to optimize flow, reduce congestion, and predict accidents.
2. **Energy Efficiency**: Neural networks monitor energy consumption patterns to optimize resource distribution and promote renewable energy usage.
3. **Public Safety**: Surveillance systems use object detection and facial recognition to identify threats and enhance security.
4. **Waste Management**: Deep learning models optimize waste collection routes and analyze recycling patterns for environmental benefits.

**Case in Point: Singapore**

Singapore has pioneered the implementation of AI-driven smart city technologies. Its smart traffic system uses deep learning to reduce congestion by dynamically adjusting traffic signals based on real-time data.

**Challenges**

- Ensuring data security and privacy in urban networks.
- Integrating AI with existing infrastructure.
- Addressing ethical concerns in surveillance and decision-making.

---

**Conclusion**

These case studies illustrate the profound impact of deep learning across industries. From autonomous vehicles navigating complex environments to AI-driven solutions in agriculture and urban management, deep learning has become a cornerstone of innovation. However, as these technologies evolve, addressing challenges such as scalability, ethical considerations, and equitable access will be critical to unlocking their full potential.

The next chapter will explore scalability and distributed systems in deep learning, discussing how to optimize performance for large-scale deployments.

14.4 Final Thoughts and Next Steps

## Chapter 14: Learning Deep Learning

Deep learning, while a sophisticated and vast field, is accessible to anyone with curiosity and determination. This chapter serves as a practical guide for embarking on the deep learning journey, from beginner resources to advanced paths. By the end, you'll have a roadmap for building your first model and insight into the next steps for growth and contribution to the field.

---

### 14.1 Resources for Beginners

Starting with deep learning can feel overwhelming due to the abundance of materials and tools. Focusing on curated, beginner-friendly resources ensures a solid foundation.

**Books and Online Courses**

- **Books**:

    1. *Deep Learning* by Ian Goodfellow, Yoshua Bengio, and Aaron Courville – A comprehensive introduction to the concepts and mathematics behind deep learning.

    2. *Python Machine Learning* by Sebastian Raschka and Vahid Mirjalili – Ideal for beginners, focusing on Python programming and its application in machine learning.

- **Online Courses**:

1. *Deep Learning Specialization* by Andrew Ng on Coursera – A structured introduction covering key topics like neural networks, CNNs, and RNNs.

2. *Fast.ai Practical Deep Learning for Coders* – Hands-on tutorials focusing on practical applications without overwhelming mathematics.

**Interactive Tools and Tutorials**

- Google Colab: A cloud-based platform for coding and running deep learning projects without requiring local hardware.

- Kaggle: Provides datasets, community support, and hands-on coding competitions for real-world applications.

**Communities and Forums**

Engaging with communities accelerates learning. Platforms like Stack Overflow, Reddit (e.g., r/MachineLearning), and specialized Slack/Discord groups provide mentorship, collaboration opportunities, and troubleshooting help.

## 14.2 Intermediate and Advanced Learning Paths

As you progress beyond beginner-level understanding, dive deeper into advanced topics, frameworks, and applications.

**Advanced Topics**

1. **Generative Models**: Understanding GANs (Generative Adversarial Networks) and Variational Autoencoders (VAEs).

2. **Transformers**: Deep dive into architectures like BERT and GPT for NLP applications.

3. **Reinforcement Learning**: Explore advanced techniques like Deep Q-Learning and Policy Gradient methods.

**Books and Research Papers**

- *Hands-On Machine Learning with Scikit-Learn, Keras, and TensorFlow* by Aurélien Géron – Covers more advanced topics with practical examples.

- *Attention Is All You Need* – The foundational paper introducing Transformers.

- *Playing Atari with Deep Reinforcement Learning* – A seminal paper in reinforcement learning applications.

**Specialized Frameworks and Tools**

1. **PyTorch and TensorFlow**: Mastering these frameworks enables you to build custom models for various use cases.

2. **Hugging Face**: Focuses on NLP with tools for working with state-of-the-art transformer models.

3. **Ray RLlib**: For scaling reinforcement learning experiments efficiently.

**Research Participation**

- Reading research papers on platforms like arXiv.

- Participating in open-source projects hosted on GitHub.

## 14.3 Building Your First Deep Learning Model

Once you're familiar with the basics, creating your first model is a rewarding milestone. Here's a step-by-step guide to help you begin:

**Step 1: Define the Problem**

Choose a simple project, such as classifying handwritten digits using the MNIST dataset or predicting housing prices.

**Step 2: Gather and Preprocess Data**

1. Obtain a dataset: Kaggle, UCI Machine Learning Repository, or open-source data libraries.

2. Data preprocessing: Clean and normalize your data to ensure consistency and compatibility with your model.

**Step 3: Select a Framework**

Use a beginner-friendly framework like TensorFlow or PyTorch. Both have extensive documentation and active communities to assist with learning.

**Step 4: Build the Model**

Define the architecture of your neural network. For example, in TensorFlow:

python

Copy code

```
from tensorflow.keras.models import Sequential

from tensorflow.keras.layers import Dense


model = Sequential([
    Dense(128, activation='relu', input_shape=(784,)),
    Dense(64, activation='relu'),
    Dense(10, activation='softmax')
```

])

## Step 4: Build the Model

Define the architecture of your neural network. For example, in TensorFlow:

```python
from tensorflow.keras.models import Sequential
from tensorflow.keras.layers import Dense

model = Sequential([
    Dense(128, activation='relu', input_shape=(784,)),
    Dense(64, activation='relu'),
    Dense(10, activation='softmax')
])
```

## Step 5: Compile and Train the Model

Specify the optimizer, loss function, and metrics.

python

Copy code

model.compile(optimizer='adam',

loss='sparse_categorical_crossentropy',

metrics=['accuracy'])

model.fit(x_train, y_train, epochs=5)

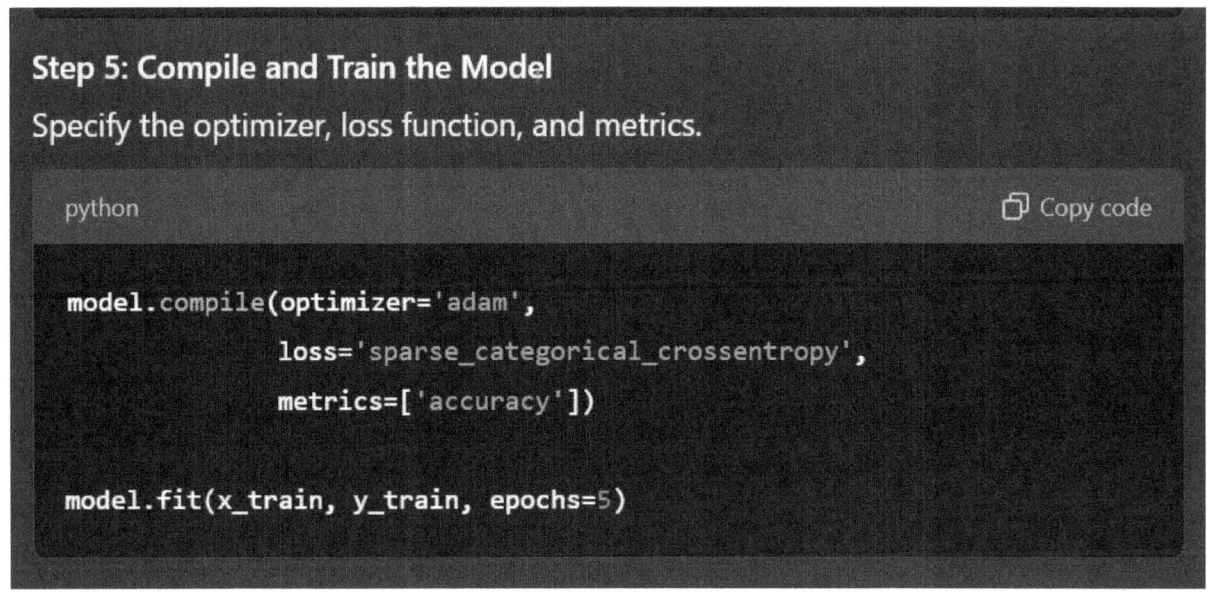

## Step 6: Evaluate and Improve

Test your model on a validation dataset. Analyze its performance and experiment with adjustments to the architecture or hyperparameters to improve accuracy.

## Step 7: Document and Share

Write about your project, share code on GitHub, and engage with the community for feedback.

---

## 14.4 Final Thoughts and Next Steps

Deep learning is an exciting and dynamic field, constantly evolving with new research, tools, and applications. As you advance:

1. **Stay Updated**: Follow AI conferences (e.g., NeurIPS, ICML, CVPR) and subscribe to newsletters or blogs for the latest trends.

2. **Experiment**: Tackle diverse datasets and problems to expand your expertise.

3. **Collaborate**: Join AI-focused hackathons or open-source initiatives to gain practical experience.

4. **Think Ethically**: Incorporate considerations of bias, fairness, and societal impact into your work.

By combining theoretical understanding with practical experimentation, you can unlock the full potential of deep learning. Whether your goal is to advance your career, contribute to groundbreaking research, or apply AI for societal benefit, the journey is as rewarding as the destination.

Embrace challenges, celebrate progress, and remain curious. With perseverance, you'll not only master deep learning but also play a role in shaping its future.

---

This chapter concludes the guide, leaving you equipped with the knowledge and inspiration to dive into deep learning. The future is bright for those willing to learn, innovate, and explore. Good luck!

**Further Resources**

To continue your journey in deep learning, leveraging the right resources can significantly enhance your understanding and practical skills. Below is a categorized list of recommended books, courses, tools, and platforms to help you grow as a deep learning enthusiast or professional.

---

**Books**

1. **Introductory Level**

    - *Deep Learning for Beginners* by Dr. Steven Cooper – An accessible guide to the foundational concepts.

    - *Python Deep Learning* by Ivan Vasilev – Introduces deep learning in Python with practical examples.

2. **Intermediate to Advanced**

    - *Deep Learning* by Ian Goodfellow, Yoshua Bengio, and Aaron Courville – A definitive textbook covering theoretical and applied aspects.

    - *Neural Networks and Deep Learning* by Michael Nielsen – A free online book focused on building neural networks from scratch.

    - *Grokking Deep Learning* by Andrew W. Trask – An engaging, hands-on introduction to understanding and building your models.

3. **Specialized Topics**

- *Hands-On Machine Learning with Scikit-Learn, Keras, and TensorFlow* by Aurélien Géron – A detailed guide to machine learning and deep learning using modern libraries.
- *Generative Deep Learning* by David Foster – Focuses on GANs, VAEs, and creative AI applications.

## Online Courses

1. **Beginner Courses**
   - *Deep Learning Specialization* by Andrew Ng (Coursera) – A highly recommended series covering the fundamentals of deep learning.
   - *Practical Deep Learning for Coders* by Fast.ai – A hands-on course with a focus on building useful models quickly.

2. **Intermediate and Advanced**
   - *Deep Reinforcement Learning* by Udacity – Dive into reinforcement learning and its applications.
   - *AI for Everyone* by Andrew Ng (Coursera) – Focuses on how AI impacts industries and prepares non-technical professionals to understand its scope.

3. **Platform-Specific**
   - *TensorFlow in Practice Specialization* by Coursera – Focuses on TensorFlow's ecosystem.
   - *PyTorch Fundamentals* by Udemy – Explores PyTorch's versatility for deep learning projects.

## Datasets for Practice

1. **General Datasets**

    - **Kaggle**: A hub for datasets and competitions to practice machine learning and deep learning.

    - **UCI Machine Learning Repository**: A collection of curated datasets for various research purposes.

2. **Specialized Domains**

    - **ImageNet**: For image classification and computer vision tasks.

    - **COCO (Common Objects in Context)**: For object detection, segmentation, and captioning.

    - **Sentiment140**: For sentiment analysis in natural language processing.

    - **MIMIC-III**: A healthcare dataset for exploring medical applications.

## Frameworks and Libraries

1. **Popular Frameworks**

    - **TensorFlow**: A robust, scalable platform with extensive documentation and support.

    - **PyTorch**: Known for its flexibility and dynamic computation graph.

    - **Keras**: A high-level API that simplifies the implementation of deep learning models.

    - **MXNet**: Lightweight and scalable, often used in edge AI applications.

2. **Domain-Specific Libraries**

    o **Hugging Face Transformers**: Specialized for NLP and transformer-based architectures.

    o **OpenCV**: For image processing and computer vision.

    o **scikit-learn**: Excellent for integrating machine learning pipelines with deep learning models.

## Tools and Platforms

1. **Cloud Computing Platforms**

    o **Google Colab**: Free GPU/TPU support for running deep learning experiments in the cloud.

    o **Amazon SageMaker**: An enterprise-level tool for building, training, and deploying models.

    o **Microsoft Azure AI**: Offers cloud services tailored for AI and deep learning workflows.

2. **Visualization Tools**

    o **TensorBoard**: For tracking metrics, visualizing model architecture, and understanding training processes.

    o **Matplotlib and Seaborn**: For creating custom visualizations of your data and results.

## Research Papers and Journals

1. **Core Concepts**
    - *Learning Representations by Backpropagating Errors* by Rumelhart et al. – Foundational paper introducing backpropagation.
    - *Attention Is All You Need* by Vaswani et al. – Introduces the transformer architecture.

2. **Application-Specific**
    - *Playing Atari with Deep Reinforcement Learning* by DeepMind – A breakthrough paper in reinforcement learning.
    - *Generative Adversarial Nets* by Ian Goodfellow et al. – Introduces GANs.

3. **Journals**
    - **Journal of Machine Learning Research (JMLR)**: Peer-reviewed articles on machine learning and deep learning advancements.
    - **Neural Information Processing Systems (NeurIPS)**: Conference proceedings containing cutting-edge research.

---

## Communities and Forums

1. **Discussion Forums**
    - **Stack Overflow**: For coding and troubleshooting help.
    - **Reddit**: Subreddits like r/MachineLearning and r/DeepLearning provide insights, news, and peer support.

2. **Meetups and Hackathons**

- **AI Meetups**: Local and virtual events for networking and knowledge sharing.
- **Kaggle Competitions**: Competitive challenges that mimic real-world problems.

**Open Source Projects**

1. **GitHub Repositories**
   - **Awesome Deep Learning**: A curated list of deep learning resources, papers, and frameworks.
   - **TensorFlow Models**: Official models developed by the TensorFlow team.
   - **PyTorch Tutorials**: Examples and guides for PyTorch users.

2. **Collaborative Projects**
   - Join open-source AI projects to contribute to real-world applications and learn from experienced developers.

**AI News and Blogs**

1. **Blogs**
   - **Distill**: Focuses on explaining complex machine learning concepts visually.
   - **Towards Data Science**: Articles ranging from beginner tutorials to cutting-edge research applications.

2. **Newsletters**
    - **The Batch by Andrew Ng**: Weekly updates on AI developments.
    - **Deep Learning Weekly**: News and resources curated for the deep learning community.

---

## Conclusion

With these resources, you can accelerate your learning, deepen your understanding, and gain practical experience in deep learning. Consistency, curiosity, and community engagement will be the pillars of your journey as you continue to explore the vast potential of deep learning.

# References

Below is a list of references cited or recommended throughout the book to provide credibility and additional resources for your deep learning journey. These include academic papers, books, websites, and online resources.

## Books

1. Ian Goodfellow, Yoshua Bengio, and Aaron Courville. *Deep Learning*. MIT Press, 2016. Link

    o A comprehensive textbook on deep learning that covers both theory and practice.

2. Michael A. Nielsen. *Neural Networks and Deep Learning*. Determination Press, 2015. Link

    o A free online book that explains the mathematics and intuition behind neural networks.

3. Aurélien Géron. *Hands-On Machine Learning with Scikit-Learn, Keras, and TensorFlow*. O'Reilly Media, 2019.

    o A practical guide to implementing machine learning and deep learning systems.

4. Andrew W. Trask. *Grokking Deep Learning*. Manning Publications, 2019.

    o An approachable book for beginners with hands-on coding exercises.

## Research Papers

1. Rumelhart, D. E., Hinton, G. E., & Williams, R. J. (1986). *Learning Representations by Backpropagating Errors*. Nature, 323(6088), 533–536.
    - The foundational paper introducing backpropagation in neural networks.
2. Vaswani, A., Shazeer, N., Parmar, N., et al. (2017). *Attention Is All You Need*. NeurIPS. Link
    - Introduced the transformer architecture, a breakthrough in deep learning for NLP.
3. Goodfellow, I., Pouget-Abadie, J., Mirza, M., et al. (2014). *Generative Adversarial Nets*. NeurIPS. Link
    - The seminal paper on Generative Adversarial Networks (GANs).
4. Mnih, V., Kavukcuoglu, K., Silver, D., et al. (2015). *Human-Level Control Through Deep Reinforcement Learning*. Nature, 518(7540), 529–533. Link
    - Demonstrates the use of deep Q-networks in reinforcement learning.

---

**Web Resources**

1. TensorFlow. Link
    - Official website for TensorFlow, a popular deep learning framework.
2. PyTorch. Link
    - Official website for PyTorch, a flexible and dynamic deep learning library.
3. UCI Machine Learning Repository. Link

- A repository of datasets for machine learning and deep learning applications.

4. Kaggle. Link

    - A platform for datasets, competitions, and collaborative learning in AI.

5. Hugging Face. Link

    - A platform providing pre-trained models and tools for natural language processing.

## Journals and Conferences

1. **Journal of Machine Learning Research (JMLR).** Link

    - A leading journal in machine learning and artificial intelligence research.

2. **Neural Information Processing Systems (NeurIPS).** Link

    - One of the most prestigious conferences for AI and deep learning research.

3. **International Conference on Learning Representations (ICLR).** Link

    - Focuses on advancements in representation learning.

## Online Courses

1. Andrew Ng. *Deep Learning Specialization.* Coursera. Link

    - A comprehensive series of courses covering deep learning fundamentals and applications.

2. Fast.ai. *Practical Deep Learning for Coders.* Link

- A hands-on course aimed at practitioners.

3. MIT OpenCourseWare. *Introduction to Deep Learning.* Link

   - A free course offered by MIT on the basics of deep learning.

---

## Datasets

1. ImageNet. Link

   - A large-scale dataset for image classification and computer vision tasks.

2. COCO (Common Objects in Context). Link

   - A dataset designed for object detection, segmentation, and captioning.

3. Sentiment140. Link

   - A dataset for sentiment analysis in social media.

4. MIMIC-III Clinical Database. Link

   - A dataset for medical research and healthcare AI applications.

---

## Communities and Forums

1. **Stack Overflow.** Link

   - A go-to platform for coding-related questions and troubleshooting.

2. **Reddit - Machine Learning Subreddit.** Link

   - Discussions on research papers, news, and AI developments.

3. **AI Meetups.** Link

- Local and virtual gatherings for networking and knowledge sharing.

---

These references will provide you with a solid foundation for deep learning and help you explore the latest advancements and applications in the field.

## Author's Note

Dear Reader,

Thank you for embarking on this journey through the fascinating world of deep learning with me. As someone deeply passionate about technology and its potential to transform our lives, writing *Deep Learning Explained: Applications, Challenges, and Opportunities* has been both a challenging and rewarding endeavor. My goal is to demystify the complexities of deep learning, making it accessible and relevant to learners, professionals, and enthusiasts alike.

In a world increasingly driven by data and algorithms, deep learning stands out as a revolutionary force, redefining how we interact with technology. From enabling self-driving cars to diagnosing diseases with unprecedented accuracy, its impact is felt across industries and borders. Yet, with great power comes great responsibility. As we push the boundaries of what machines can achieve, it is crucial to understand not just the opportunities but also the ethical implications and challenges.

This book is not just about the mechanics of deep learning but also about its broader implications—how it is reshaping industries, solving real-world problems, and presenting us with moral and societal dilemmas that we must address thoughtfully. I hope to inspire you to explore the field further, whether you're building your first neural network, deploying models in real-world settings, or pondering the ethical challenges of AI.

A special thank you goes to the researchers, developers, and pioneers who continue to advance this field, often in ways that seem like science fiction brought to life. Your work has provided the foundation for the ideas and examples in this book.

Lastly, to my readers—your curiosity and drive for understanding are what make books like this meaningful. Whether you're a beginner taking your first steps into the world of AI or an experienced practitioner seeking to deepen your knowledge, I hope this book offers valuable insights and inspires your next steps.

Happy learning and innovating!

Warm regards,

**Oluchi Ike**